The Book
of
Druthers

The Book of Druthers

of

Druthers

???

by
The Druthers Sisters

Linda Ross Aldy, Annetta Jean Allred, Ann Homer Cook,
Beverly Keaton Smith, and Catherine Hamilton Stroud

QUAIL RIDGE PRESS

Library of Congress Cataloging-in-Publication Data

The book of druthers : when given your "druthers," the choices you make can
illuminate, enlighten, amuse, and definitley entertain! : a unique way to deepen
your relationship with yourself, friends, and family / by the Drutehrs Sisters ;
Linda Ross Aldy ... [et al.].
     p. cm.
   ISBN 1-893062-51-1
   1. Values clarification. I. Aldy, Linda Ross, 1952- II. Druthers Sisiters (Group)
BJ66.B66 2003
153.8'3—dc22   2003058475

9 8 7 6 5 4 3 2 1
FIRST EDITION
ISBN 1-893062-51-1

Art direction by Stacey Deen Griffith, www.tidaldev.com

Printed in the United States of America.

QUAIL RIDGE PRESS
P. O. Box 123 ♦ Brandon, MS 39043 ♦ 1-800-343-1583
info@quailridge.com ♦ www.quailridge.com

DEDICATION

The Druthers Sisters dedicate this book to everyone who enjoys Druthering. We honor your creativity and respect your desire to learn more about yourself and others. May you think deeply, laugh loudly and expand your horizons beyond your wildest dreams.

ACKNOWLEDGMENTS

The Druthers Sisters wish to express heartfelt gratitude to everyone at Quail Ridge Press in Brandon, Mississippi who worked with us on *The Book of Druthers*. We are forever grateful to publisher Barney McKee for his ongoing support and enthusiasm. To Sheila Williams, associate publisher, we say thank you for your dedication to making this book happen. We applaud book designer, Stacey Deen Griffith who proved herself to be an expert. We also thank all of our friends and family members who offered us encouragement along the way. Last but not least, The Druthers Sisters give a great big thank you to each other. Without the effort of our group as a whole, this book would not have happened.

Introduction

druth·ers (drŭth'rz) – A choice or preference.

In the South, a popular phrase begins like this: If I had my druthers, I would... (fill in the blank with what you would most like to do). It's how many southerners express a preference regarding all types of situations.

Sometimes we can't have our druthers. That's just the way life goes. Fortunately, The Druthers Sisters have created a remedy for this situation. Whenever you answer the questions in this book, you are guaranteed to always have your Druthers. Free yourself from limitations and let your mind run wild as you reflect on the thought-provoking questions.

Would you druther

. . . see the future

. . . remember every minute of the past

. . . live strictly in the present, every minute of every day

Which answer appeals to you? Why did you choose that answer? What made the other choices unappealing? Are you surprised by your answer? Which answer would your friends choose?

The Journey: How We Began "Druthering"

We stumbled onto all of this innocently. It was not our
intention to name ourselves The Druthers Sisters or to write
The Book of Druthers. It just happened.

In the beginning, five women—Ann, Annetta, Beverly,
Cathy and Linda—settled into a warm and cozy group. We
met regularly to explore our thoughts and feelings, wishes
and dreams, concerns and heartaches, as well as our joys
and triumphs. Ann, our leader, appropriately named us the
"journey group," since we joined together to focus on living
life authentically.

One evening, Cathy told us about a game she played with
some friends while waiting for a concert to begin. The
instructions were simple: You are asked a question and pro-
vided with three possible answers. You must choose one of
the answers and then explain why. Listening to Cathy's story
made us all want to state our Druthers to the following ques-
tion. The question seems easy enough, but is it? There are
many things to consider about each choice.

Would you druther

   . . . keep a secret

   . . . tell just one person

   . . . tell everyone

We had so much fun Druthering that right then and there, we decided to kick off all our meetings with a Druthers question. We took turns thinking of questions, and we eagerly listened to each other's responses. Much to our surprise, we could not stop writing and answering our own Druthers questions. The thought process of writing and answering the questions captivated us. It was fun and enlightening to share our thoughts. We were hooked.

When we realized that we were addicted to Druthers, Linda suggested that we write *The Book of Druthers*. After all, it would not have been very nice of us to keep The Druthers Experience a secret. We wanted to share it with everyone.

How to Use **The Book of Druthers** *with a Group*

The Book of Druthers can be used by two or more people. The questions promise to unleash lively conversations at parties, on road trips with friends and family, or any other kind of social gathering.

There is one guideline to follow when using *The Book of Druthers*: select an answer from the three options listed. If you dislike all of the choices, determine which option you are least opposed to and explain why.

There are no right or wrong answers when playing a round of Druthers. Since everyone is different, responses to the Druthers questions will vary. Remember, this is not a competitive activity. No one is keeping score. Each person has a right to express an authentic opinion, and it is important to be open-minded about all responses. This leads to a fun and entertaining Druthers experience as well as a window of opportunity to peer into your beliefs or the preferences of those who participate in a round of Druthers with you.

Starting a Group of Your Own

The Book of Druthers provides tangible evidence that the unlikely is likely to happen when people gather on a regular basis to nurture and applaud each other. This book is a testament to group power, visioning, and the strength of perseverance.

With a little effort, anyone can take advantage of the positive energy which is generated from being involved with a group of supportive and cooperative people. If you doubt your ability to create a group, remember, it only takes two people who are willing to make a commitment to one another. Bigger is not necessarily better. If you are not sure about topics to discuss, turn to *The Book of Druthers*. Simply toss out a few questions and dance along with the conversation as it starts to move.

$\mathcal{H}$ow to Use **The Book of Druthers** Alone

The Book of Druthers gives you an opportunity to think aloud and speak freely with others or to reflect privately by using a journal. If you prefer not to share your answers for Druthers questions with others, try keeping a journal of your responses in order to gain insight about yourself. All you need for this is a notebook, a pen, and a little quiet time. The following questions will help you explore your answers in depth: Did my answer come quickly or was I torn between two? What did I reject and why? What appeals to me about my choice? Is there some special memory or early ambition or desire connected to my response? Why did I choose my answer? What kind of mood was I in when I answered (playful, sad, happy, introspective, searching)?

$\mathcal{T}$he Druthers Sisters

The Druthers Sisters love to Druther. So we have included some of our responses to Druthers questions on the following pages. It was impossible to include all of the conversation and laughter that evolved from each question into a small space, so the replies are a condensed version of our original responses. Notice that none of us ever chose the same answer for the same reason. This shows there are no right or wrong answers to the Druther questions. Druthering is a time to proudly let your individuality shine.

When Druthering, we strive to be honest and remove all barriers from our thought process. We go to a place where we can stretch our minds, spread our wings and strut our stuff. We laugh, cry, hoot, holler, clap, cheer, gasp with shock, rant, rave, share secrets, and reflect. We learn about ourselves and each other. Above all else, we have fun.

We hope that Druthering will take you to a similar place. May your life be enriched by finally finding a way to always have your Druthers.

The Book of Druthers

1   *If you were attending an exclusive party in the most gorgeous home in town and had to use the restroom facilities, would you **druther***

    . . . accomplish your business and leave the room

    . . . snoop just a little in the cabinets

    . . . do a total search

2   *Your worst enemy is going to die without a kidney transplant, would you **druther***

    . . . give one of your kidneys

    . . . find another donor

    . . . do nothing

3   *Would you **druther** be*

    . . . an antique mantle clock

    . . . a time clock

    . . . an alarm clock

4 *Would you **druther** be*

   . . . an animal mask worn by a tribal chieftain

   . . . a Mardi Gras mask worn to a ball
on Fat Tuesday

   . . . a Halloween mask worn by a small child

5 *Would you **druther** be a*

   . . . mountain bike

   . . . pair of hiking shoes

   . . . backpack

6 *Would you **druther** be a*

   . . . golf ball that rolls and flies around a sunny
golf course in Phoenix, Arizona

   . . . bowling ball which belongs to a famous,
professional bowler

   . . . crystal ball that tells the future and
gives advice

7 *Would you druther be a*

   ... party hat that emits a festive mood
   ... wool hat that provides safety and warmth
   ... cowboy hat filled with promises of adventure

8 *Would you druther*

   ... eat
   ... sleep
   ... exercise

9 *Would you druther eat a*

   ... healthy piece of fruit
   ... piece of chocolate from Switzerland
   ... bowl of popcorn

10 **W**ould you **druther** be a

  • • • frisbee that sails back and forth between two
    people having fun

  • • • kite that entertains and relieves stress

  • • • volleyball that is the center of attention in a
    group of people

11 **W**ould you **druther** decorate your home in

  • • • country style

  • • • antiques

  • • • contemporary style

12 **W**ould you **druther** be

  • • • a Barbie® doll that never worries about
    being unattractive

  • • • a rag doll that bends and folds into all
    positions

  • • • an antique doll on public display

13 *Would you **druther** be a*

- . . . monitor displaying data and graphics
- . . . printer that prints data and graphics
- . . . computer that computes

14 *Would you **druther** be*

- . . . a microwave that quickly zaps
- . . . an oven that slowly bakes and broils
- . . . an outdoor grill which sends the smell of delicious food throughout the neighborhood

15 *Would you **druther** be a*

- . . . coffee pot which serves morning coffee
- . . . tea pot which serves afternoon tea
- . . . flower pot full of purple pansies

16 *Would you **druther** be a*
- ... sailboat that relies on wind
- ... fishing boat that uses a trolling motor
- ... ski boat that depends on a high-powered motor

17 *Would you **druther** be a*
- ... washing machine spinning and cleaning
- ... clothes dryer tumbling and drying
- ... sewing machine creating and humming

18 *Would you **druther** be a*
- ... flashlight that lights up the darkness during emergencies
- ... motion light that requires activity to light up the darkness
- ... skylight that is totally dependent on the sun

19 *Would you druther be*

... a tree that grows delicious healthy oranges in Florida

... an artificial Christmas tree with twinkling, multi-colored lights

... a huge weeping willow tree that lives by a peaceful lake

20 *Would you druther be a*

... bird cage in a pet store

... bird's nest high in a tree in the woods

... bird bath in a church courtyard

21 *Would you druther be a*

... lion tamer

... computer wizard

... spy

22 *Would you **druther** receive a*

. . . pedicure

. . . manicure

. . . facial

23 *Would you **druther** have*

. . . deep blue eyes

. . . warm brown eyes

. . . mysterious green eyes

24 *Would you **druther** have*

. . . a pierced naval

. . . a tattoo

. . . green hair

25 *If you could make the headlines, would you* **druther** *see*

   ... Local Writer Wins Pulitzer Prize

   ... Successful Entrepreneur Establishes Endowment

   ... Local Photographer Receives Grand Prize for *National Geographic* Cover

26 *Would you* **druther** *eat*

   ... lasagne in an Italian restaurant

   ... enchiladas in a Mexican restaurant

   ... sushi in a Japanese restaurant

27 *Would you* **druther** *receive*

   ... a ruby ring

   ... a sapphire necklace

   ... an emerald bracelet

?

28 *Would you druther*

... water ski in Florida

... snow ski in Austria

... jet ski on Lake Michigan

29 *Would you druther*

... speak in front of 5,000 people

... sing in front of 5,000 people

... dance the Twist on a stage in front of 5,000 people

30 *Would you druther be more like*

... your mother

... your father

... a sibling

31 *Would you* **druther** *drink coffee from a*

... mug

... china cup

... Styrofoam cup

32 *Would you* **druther** *be a*

... child's tire swing

... tire on the winning car at the Indianapolis 500

... tire flower planter

33 *On a rainy cold day, would you* **druther**

... stay in bed reading

... watch movies at home

... make soup

34 *Would you **druther** spend a day*
- ... lying in the sun on a sandy beach
- ... hiking the Appalachian Trail
- ... visiting with friends

35 *Would you **druther** change your*
- ... appearance
- ... intelligence level
- ... talents

36 *Would you **druther** win*
- ... an Oscar®
- ... an Emmy
- ... a Grammy®

37 Would you *druther* be a

. . . big fish in a little pond

. . . little fish in a big pond

. . . gold fish in a glass bowl

38 Would you *druther* be

. . . a rag rug, frayed around the edges, in a family room

. . . an Oriental rug from Turkey, below an ornate dining table

. . . a grass rug in Tahiti, covering a cottage floor

39 Would you *druther* be a

. . . wild rose growing in a field

. . . rose in a large public garden

. . . rose in a bride's bouquet

?

40 *W*ould you **druther** relax after a grueling day with

. . . a bubble bath surrounded by scented candles

. . . a good book

. . . an energizing workout

The bubble bathers had a tough time believing anybody could choose anything else. No one could understand Beverly's choice!

Annetta: Good book, because I like to shower and then get into bed with a good book.
Linda: Bubble baths are boring to me. I would read a book.
Cathy: A bubble bath. It so relaxing and nurturing.
Ann: A bubble bath. Of course, then I get in bed with a good book!
Bev: An energizing workout. The endorphins created by a workout do wonders for me.

41 *Would you druther be a*

. . . gondola in Venice, Italy

. . . ski lift in Aspen, Colorado

. . . roller coaster at Walt Disney World®

42 *Would you druther be a*

. . . hardwood floor in an old antebellum home

. . . showroom floor at a car dealership

. . . dance floor at a night club

43 *Would you druther be*

. . . cotton candy served at a big carnival

. . . hard candy in a glass bowl in someone's office

. . . chocolate candy found in a heart shaped box
   on a bedside table

44 *Would you **druther** be a*

... college textbook

... city phone book

... guest book at a bed and breakfast inn

45 *Would you **druther** be a*

... speedy fire truck

... forceful and loud siren

... flexible water hose

46 *Would you **druther** be*

... Peter Pan who never grows up

... Wendy who is responsible and mature

... Tinker Bell who is small and magical

47 *Would you* **druther**

- ... have BOTOX® injections
- ... have liposuction
- ... age naturally

48 *Would you* **druther**

- ... win the lottery and achieve instant wealth
- ... win an award which leads you to become nationally recognized
- ... anonymously build a children's wing on a hospital

49 *Would you* **druther**

- ... watch a magician who mystifies all with unexplainable acts of magic
- ... be a magician who entertains audiences around the world
- ... be a magician's assistant who knows all of the tricks

50 Would you druther

... go to the zoo alone

... walk in a forest alone

... go shopping alone

51 Would you druther be a

... candy cane, decorative and festive

... walking cane, sturdy and functional

... sugar cane, alive with sweetness

52 Would you druther hear a

... nursery rhyme that entertains

... lullaby that puts a child to sleep

... fairy tale that invokes the imagination

53 *Would you **druther** be*

... mud that children play in

... dirt that flowers grow in

... clay that molds into various objects

54 *Would you **druther** be a*

... cricket, chirping and hopping

... minnow, swimming and growing

... worm, regenerating

55 *Would you **druther** be*

... a rainbow after a rainy day

... blue sky full of bright sunshine

... a white cloud shaped like an angel

?

56 *Would you **druther***

   ... interpret dreams

   ... speak all languages

   ... have ESP

57 *If you could only have one book,
    would you **druther** it be*

   ... spiritual

   ... reference

   ... poetry

58 *If you had to live inside a shape,
    would you **druther** it be a*

   ... circle

   ... heart

   ... star

59 *Would you **druther** be a*

... Laundromat® in the Vatican

... doormat at The White House

... placemat at Madonna's table

60 *Would you **druther** paint*

... portraits

... abstracts

... landscapes

61 *Would you **druther** enjoy a*

... sunset

... sunrise

... starry night

?

62 *Would you* **druther**

- . . . keep a secret
- . . . tell just one person
- . . . tell everyone

63 *Would you* **druther** *endure*

- . . . boot camp
- . . . college rush
- . . . wilderness camp

64 *Would you* **druther** *have*

- . . . adventure
- . . . peace
- . . . wealth

65 **W**ould you *druther*

   ... stop a fight

   ... start a fight

   ... win a fight

66 **W**ould you *druther* use a

   ... fountain pen

   ... conductor's baton

   ... paintbrush

67 **W**ould you *druther* design a

   ... picnic basket

   ... fruit basket

   ... flower girl's basket

?

68 *Would you druther be*

- . . . an anchor, providing stability and keeping your boat where you want it to be

- . . . a paddle, moving your boat forward, but not without your effort and hard work

- . . . a sail, that when billowy and full of wind, will move your boat effortlessly forward

69 *Would you druther*

- . . . see the future

- . . . remember every minute of the past

- . . . live strictly in the present, every minute of the day

70 *Would you druther*

- . . . receive a life sentence

- . . . receive the death penalty

- . . . live with the guilt

71 *If you could find a cure for one disease, would you **druther** conquer*

... heart disease

... cancer

... AIDS

72 *If you won a million bucks, would you **druther***

... share it with others

... spend freely

... save and invest all of it

73 *Would you **druther** be*

... scissors that cut

... a rock that crushes

... paper that covers

74 *Would you druther*

   . . . go to a party

   . . . plan a party

   . . . host a party

75 *Would you druther cover windows with*

   . . . lush, velvety drapes

   . . . nothing

   . . . wooden shutters

76 *Would you druther have*

   . . . money

   . . . fame

   . . . love

77 *If* you could only have one item with which to decorate your home, would you **druther** choose

... sea shells

... glass bottles

... baskets

78 *Would* you **druther** be

... hot

... cold

... wet

79 *Would* you **druther** marry for

... money

... love

... power

80 *If you could be any age, would you **druther** be*

... 10 years old

... 21 years old

... your present age

This one generated some lively discussion about the pros and cons of each of the ages.

Annetta: Knowing that I can't go back and take what I know now, I choose to be my present age.

Linda: I would love to have another 10-year-old summer. But, I wouldn't want to change anything from the path that I've taken.

Cathy: I'd be 21. I missed my twenties completely because I studied the whole time. I would take advantage of a second chance to do something different.

Ann: I'll stay with my present age because all of the major decisions in my life have already been made.

Bev: I'll stay with my present age. It's a nice place to be.

81 *Would you druther*

... travel the world in 80 days

... visit your favorite country for 80 days

... stay in a monastery for 80 days

82 *Would you druther*

... walk the great wall of China

... hike the Appalachian trail

... float along the Amazon

83 *Would you druther live in a*

... haunted house

... hippie commune

... tent in the wilderness

84 *Would you **druther** experience anger from*
- . . . your mother
- . . . your best friend
- . . . your boss

85 *Would you **druther** live a life like*
- . . . Oprah
- . . . Mother Theresa
- . . . June Cleaver

86 *Would you **druther** lose your*
- . . . wallet
- . . . baby ring
- . . . appointment calendar

87 *If* you wanted to meet a potential date, would you **druther** meet someone from

. . . an ad you placed in the personals

. . . a local singles gathering place

. . . a blind date

88 *Would* you **druther**

. . . go barefooted

. . . wear socks

. . . wear slippers

89 *At* Christmas would you **druther**

. . . be at home with your immediate family

. . . be at a relative's home visiting extended family

. . . take an exotic vacation with your family

90 *Would you **druther** sleep between*

   . . . silk sheets

   . . . cotton sheets

   . . . flannel sheets

91 *Would you **druther** have a house full of*

   . . . children

   . . . pets

   . . . friends

92 *Would you **druther** overcome your fear of*

   . . . snakes

   . . . public speaking

   . . . audit by the IRS

93 *Would you druther be*

. . . an electric blanket that keeps people warm

. . . a handmade quilt that is a keepsake

. . . a down comforter that decorates the top of a bed

94 *Would you druther be a*

. . . make-up kiss after an argument

. . . kiss on a baby's cheek

. . . kiss on the Blarney Stone

95 *Would you druther wear a*

. . . blue denim shirt

. . . silk blouse

. . . wool sweater

?

96 *Would you druther*

. . . be in a wedding

. . . attend a wedding

. . . direct a wedding

97 *Would you druther*

. . . play horseshoes

. . . put horseshoes on a horse

. . . hang a horseshoe over your door for good luck

98 *For Thanksgiving, would you druther*

. . . hunt for your turkey in the wild

. . . raise a live turkey to slaughter and cook

. . . buy a frozen turkey at the grocery store

99 *Would you druther* marry

. . . at age 20

. . . at age 30

. . . at age 40

100 *Would you druther* answer a

. . . job interview question

. . . newspaper interview question

. . . druther question

101 *Would you druther* attend a

. . . wild bachelorette party

. . . family reunion

. . . large party given by a close friend

102 *Would you **druther** be without your*

- ... home telephone service
- ... internet service
- ... cell phone

103 *Would you **druther** communicate by use of*

- ... email
- ... U.S. Mail
- ... telephone

104 *Would you **druther***

- ... have children of your own
- ... remain childless by choice
- ... adopt a child

105 *If you had to carry something heavy up the stairs, would you druther carry*

... groceries

... luggage

... a child

106 *Would you druther wear a*

... leather coat

... wool coat

... mink coat

107 *If you knew you were dying, would you druther tell*

... only your family members

... your family and close friends

... no one

108 Would you *druther* be in

. . . a stadium full of football fans

. . . a coliseum full of ice skating fans

. . . an auditorium full of opera fans

109 Would you *druther* be a

. . . stage for a choir

. . . prop for a play

. . . podium for a public speaker

110 Would you *druther* be a

. . . cotton field

. . . strawberry field

. . . football field

111 *Would you **druther** be a*

- . . . credit card
- . . . greeting card
- . . . discount card

112 *Would you **druther** be a*

- . . . deck over a pool
- . . . garden patio in the French Quarter
- . . . porch swing

113 *Would you **druther** be in the presence of a*

- . . . prophet
- . . . politician
- . . . poet

?

114 *Would you **druther** relax in your living room on a*

- . . . velour couch
- . . . leather couch
- . . . chintz couch

115 *Would you **druther***

- . . . be bored at a high paying job that only requires working 40 hours a week
- . . . work 60+ hours at a job you love for moderate pay
- . . . be self-employed with flexible hours and uncertain income

116 *Would you **druther** be a*

- . . . creative person with lots of responsibilities
- . . . carefree person with few responsibilities
- . . . cautious person with moderate responsibilities

117 Would you *druther* be a

. . . movie critic

. . . restaurant critic

. . . critic of performance art

118 Would you *druther* be a

. . . journalist for *The Washington Post*

. . . writer for *People Magazine*

. . . columnist for *The Wall Street Journal*

119 Would you *druther* work with

. . . adults

. . . children

. . . animals

120 *W*ould you **druther** be a

. . . blonde

. . . brunette

. . . redhead

This one didn't create too much conversation, but we loved Ann's new phrase, "Since I'm Druthering."

Annetta: I'd druther have big red hair. I want it to be thick because my hair has always been thin.

Cathy: I'd be a brunette with crystal blue eyes and no freckles!

Linda: I'll stick to being a blonde. I have no desire to change it.

Ann: Since I'm Druthering, I'll take red hair, green eyes and porcelain skin.

Bev: I'll stay a redhead. It suits me.

121 **W**ould you **druther** be the editor of

    . . . *Vanity Fair*

    . . . *People Magazine*

    . . . *Sports Illustrated*

122 **A**s a doctor, would you **druther** specialize in

    . . . babies

    . . . infectious diseases

    . . . surgery

123 **W**ould you **druther** write a

    . . . great novel

    . . . hit song

    . . . Broadway play

124 *Would you **druther** receive your fortune from*

   ... luck

   ... hard work

   ... inheritance

125 *At work, would you **druther** use your*

   ... brains

   ... hands

   ... back

126 *If you were a physical trainer,*
*would you **druther** train people for*

   ... the Masters

   ... an NFL Championship game

   ... Wimbledon

127 *If you were just starting your education, would you druther study*

... liberal arts

... business education

... science and technology

128 *Would you druther work at*

... a tourist shop in Gatlinburg, Tennessee

... a university in California

... an investment firm in New York City

129 *On the job, would you druther be like*

... a hare, symbolizing speed

... an owl, symbolizing wisdom

... a tortoise, symbolizing persistence

?

130 **W**ould you **druther** be an expert in

. . . math

. . . literature

. . . geography

131 **W**ould you **druther** be a successful

. . . seamstress

. . . photographer

. . . baker

132 **W**ould you **druther** be a

. . . two-wheel bicycle

. . . four-wheel car

. . . 18-wheel truck

133 *W*ould you **druther** be a fire

. . . hydrant

. . . extinguisher

. . . escape

134 *W*ould you **druther** be

. . . a gas pump

. . . an air pump

. . . a water pump

135 *W*ould you **druther** be a

. . . postage stamp

. . . date stamp

. . . stamp of approval

?

136 Would you *druther* be

- . . . a dictionary
- . . . a thesaurus
- . . . an encyclopedia

137 Would you *druther* have staff meetings in a

- . . . traditional conference room
- . . . coffee house
- . . . retreat center

138 When going to work, would you *druther* wear

- . . . a business suit
- . . . jeans or shorts
- . . . khakis

139 *At the end of the day, would you **druther** leave your desk at work*

. . . cluttered

. . . neatly organized with in and out bins

. . . clean with nothing on top

140 *Would you **druther***

. . . keep your current career

. . . change your career

. . . retire

141 *Would you **druther** spend*

. . . more time at work

. . . less time at work

. . . the same amount of time at work

142 *W*ould you **druther** be known for

. . . ethics

. . . creativity

. . . deal-making

143 *W*ould you **druther** be

. . . a dolphin swimming in the ocean

. . . an eagle soaring over mountains

. . . a cat napping in a sunny window

144 *W*ould you **druther** travel in

. . . the United States

. . . Europe

. . . Africa

145 *Would you **druther** spend*

- . . . one hour building a sandcastle on the beach
- . . . four months building your dream house
- . . . twenty-five years building a savings account of one million dollars

146 *Would you **druther** ride in*

- . . . a colorful hot air balloon, peacefully and slowly sailing the skies
- . . . a helicopter providing rescue service
- . . . Airforce One

147 *Would you **druther** pretend to be a*

- . . . conductor of a magnificent invisible orchestra
- . . . go-go dancer wiggling to the beat of the 60s
- . . . sultry model, cat-walking down a long runway

?

148 **W**ould you **druther** be a

  . . . meadow of spring flowers in France

  . . . tulip farm in Holland

  . . . cotton farm in India

149 **W**ould you **druther** be a

  . . . wool sweater

  . . . silk shirt

  . . . cotton T-shirt

150 **I**f you were a superhero, would you **druther** be

  . . . Wonder Woman

  . . . Superman

  . . . Spider-Man

151 Would you *druther* be a plant that

   ... blooms

   ... heals

   ... is exceptionally rare

152 Would you *druther* be a

   ... flower child

   ... Hell's angel

   ... preppie

153 Would you *druther* receive an invitation to a

   ... cocktail party

   ... child's birthday party

   ... wedding shower

154 *For one day, would you **druther** be*
- ... Queen
- ... President
- ... Pope

155 *As a child, would you **druther** have had a*
- ... pony
- ... secret garden
- ... tree house

156 *Would you **druther** have a visit from*
- ... the sandman
- ... your fairy godmother
- ... a genie in a bottle

157 **W**ould you **druther** discover a

. . . long-lost possession

. . . pirate's treasure chest

. . . safe full of cash

158 **W**ould you **druther** spend the evening searching through

. . . a basement

. . . an attic

. . . a closet

159 **W**ould you **druther** be a

. . . guest room

. . . storage room

. . . dressing room

?

160 Would you *druther* be a

... mirror which reflects only beauty

... windowpane through which you see the truth

... fun-house mirror which distorts

This one created a lot of laughter. We interrupted each other constantly and challenged each other's choices.

Linda: Windowpane of truth because a window is clear. You can see beauty as well as reality which may not always be what you want to see, but rather what you need to see.

Annetta: Mirror which reflects only beauty. But I know if I chose the fun-house mirror, it could make us look skinnier and younger.

Ann: Mirror which reflects only beauty, since there is comfort to be found in beauty.

Cathy: Windowpane of truth. I hate untruth and lies.

Bev: A fun-house mirror which distorts because sometimes we need an escape from reality.

161 *Would you **druther** be a*

. . . ballet dancer, graceful and flexible

. . . tap dancer, energetic and happy

. . . ballroom dancer, smooth and eloquent

162 *Would you **druther***

. . . dance on a cloud

. . . ride on a comet

. . . walk on the moon

163 *Would you **druther** find a thrill by*

. . . skydiving from a plane

. . . hang gliding off a mountain

. . . parasailing over deep blue water

?

164 *W*hen redecorating your house, would you **druther**

   ... change the paint or wallpaper

   ... buy new furniture

   ... install hardwood floors

165 *W*ould you **druther** master the

   ... guitar

   ... piano

   ... flute

166 *W*ould you **druther** change your

   ... height

   ... laugh

   ... eye color

167 *Would you druther look at*

... George Clooney

... Robert Redford

... Mel Gibson

168 *Would you druther look at*

... Michelle Pfeiffer

... Catherine Zeta-Jones

... Lauren Bacall

169 *Would you druther*

... attend a survival camp in the gorgeous lands of northern Canada

... travel Europe on a strict budget, staying in hostels

... work on an African safari team

170 **W**ould you **druther** work a

. . . jigsaw puzzle

. . . crossword puzzle

. . . seek and find puzzle

171 **W**ould you **druther** play

. . . Scrabble®

. . . Monopoly®

. . . Solitaire

172 **W**ould you **druther** find a key to a

. . . safe deposit box

. . . hotel room

. . . music box

?

173 *Would you **druther** be*

... a cathedral

... a science museum

... an art gallery

174 *Would you **druther** have been*

... delivered by a stork

... evolved from a monkey

... the result of immaculate conception

175 *Would you **druther** go to*

... Mars

... Venus

... a marriage counselor

176 **W**ould you **druther** be a

... giraffe, not afraid to stick out your neck

... hippopotamus, not afraid to open your mouth

... monkey, not afraid to swing by your own tail

177 **I**f you had to choose a different family, would you **druther** live with

... The Flintstones

... The Simpsons

... The Munsters

178 **W**ould you **druther** play a

... card game

... board game

... computer game

?

179 *Would you **druther** throw darts at*

. . . a dart board in a competitive game

. . . an enemy's picture

. . . balloons and try to win a prize

180 *Would you **druther** watch a*

. . . medical show

. . . legal show

. . . comedy sitcom

181 *Would you **druther** swim in a*

. . . clean, blue lake

. . . deserted Olympic-sized pool

. . . crowded ocean of the Gulf of Mexico

182 **W**ould you **druther** stand in a long line to get a

... ticket to see your favorite performer

... boarding pass for a flight to your favorite destination

... ticket for a ride at an amusement park

183 **A**t a parade, would you **druther**

... march in the parade

... watch the parade

... ride on a float in the parade

184 **W**ould you **druther** go

... fishing in the spring

... deer hunting in the winter

... swimming in the summer

185 *Would you* **druther** *have*
  . . . bats in the belfry
  . . . ghosts in the hallway
  . . . squirrels in the attic

186 *Would you* **druther** *play*
  . . . hopscotch
  . . . red rover
  . . . hide and seek

187 *Would you* **druther** *ride a*
  . . . Ferris wheel
  . . . roller coaster
  . . . water slide

188 *Would you **druther** be*

. . . an only child

. . . an identical twin

. . . one of several siblings

189 *Would you **druther***

. . . have your own name

. . . choose a new name

. . . be named after a relative

190 *Would you **druther** be*

. . . a member of the audience

. . . an actor on the stage

. . . the stage director behind the scenes

191 *Would you **druther** have a room painted*

. . . orange

. . . purple

. . . chartreuse

192 *Would you **druther***

. . . be the subject of the news

. . . watch the news

. . . report the news

193 *Would you **druther** shop at*

. . . the mall for designer labels

. . . discount stores

. . . Goodwill

?

194 *Would you* **druther**

   . . . square dance

   . . . waltz

   . . . tango

195 *In a storm, would you* **druther** *be the*

   . . . lightning

   . . . thunder

   . . . rain

196 *In a storm, would you* **druther** *rely on*

   . . . an umbrella

   . . . a raincoat

   . . . rubber boots

197 Would you *druther* donate your

- ... time
- ... money
- ... blood

198 Would you *druther* be a sink

- ... in a ceramic studio
- ... used by a surgeon before performing surgery
- ... in a photographer's dark room

199 In the ecosystem, would you *druther* be

- ... leaves
- ... roots
- ... stem

?

200 **W**ould you **druther** people remember your

... smile

... hair

... eyes

This one created a somber mood because one of our group was dealing with a loss. We began to realize how our choices in life, even in something as simple as our Druthers choices, can be affected by what we are experiencing.

Linda: Eyes are the window of your soul. A smile can be faked.

Annetta: I remember so many people in my yearbook saying I had a sweet smile, so I will go with the smile.

Cathy: Smile. I want to be remembered as a happy person who makes people laugh.

Ann: Eyes show the real person. You can't fake what shows through your eyes, but a smile can be faked.

Bev: Smiles sprinkle the world with joy, even during the saddest times.

201 Would you *druther* be

. . . eyeglasses

. . . sunglasses

. . . goggles

202 Would you *druther* be covered with

. . . feathers

. . . skin

. . . fur

203 Would you *druther* look for a

. . . street sign

. . . neon sign

. . . for sale sign

204 *W*ould you **druther** be a

. . . gold medal winner in the Olympics

. . . gold digger

. . . goldsmith

205 *F*or personal entertainment,
would you **druther** have a

. . . a television

. . . a stereo

. . . books

206 *I*n your home, would you **druther** have

. . . a refrigerator

. . . indoor plumbing

. . . heat

207 Would you *druther* have a pet

 . . . snake

 . . . bird

 . . . gold fish

208 Would you *druther* go to a

 . . . movie

 . . . concert

 . . . play

209 Would you *druther* go to a

 . . . baseball game

 . . . football game

 . . . hockey game

?

210 *Would you **druther** be a*

- ... pink flamingo in an upscale seaside shop
- ... glass unicorn in an exclusive New York department store
- ... hand-thrown pottery pig in a craft shop

211 *Would you **druther***

- ... speak fluent Spanish on a tour to Spain
- ... use sign language while visiting a school for the deaf
- ... read Arabic on a tour to the Holy Lands

212 *Would you **druther** write*

- ... the #1 book on the *New York Times* Best-Seller List
- ... a play in which your child is to be the star
- ... the most sought-after college textbook on insects of America

213 *If you could relive your high school years, would you druther*

   ... do it the same way

   ... be a better student

   ... be more popular

214 *Would you druther be the up-and-coming*

   ... movie star

   ... politician

   ... writer

215 *Would you druther be a*

   ... Kentucky Derby winner

   ... kiddie pony at a fair

   ... cowboy's winning cutting horse at a rodeo

216 *If you won a check for a million dollars, would you **druther** purchase a*

... mansion for a happy family

... school for exceptional math and science students

... rustic chapel in the woods

217 *If you were an egg, would you **druther** be a*

... richly dyed Easter egg in a child's basket

... fresh brown egg in a basket on the way to market

... Fabergé® egg displayed in a glass basket in a store window

218 *If you were the new baby in the family, would you **druther** be the*

... first born who was named all the old family names due to wealth

... middle child of a hippie family, named after a season

... youngest child in a family of twelve whose name starts with the same letter as the other eleven

219 **W**ould you **druther** *spend the day*

... at a spa with friends

... shopping with your mother

... fishing with your lover

220 **W**ould you **druther** *get your news*

... by watching the 6 p.m. news on television

... reading the daily paper

... through the gossip circle

221 **W**ould you **druther** *work at your favorite job for*

... only four hours a day for six days a week

... ten hours a day for four days a week

... eight to five for only six months of each year

222 *If your best friend were in a relationship with someone you knew was being unfaithful, would you* **druther**

. . . keep quiet about it

. . . behave as if you did not like the person

. . . be brutally honest about the situation

223 *Would you* **druther** *spend your vacation*

. . . on a cruise

. . . on a beach

. . . at home working on projects you've been wanting to catch up on

224 *If you were unable to take care of yourself due to illness, would you* **druther**

. . . have family move in with you

. . . move to some type of residential care

. . . move in with family

225 *If you are doing community service, would you* **druther**

- . . . feed the hungry at a homeless shelter
- . . . build a house for a needy family
- . . . canvass your neighborhood for clothes and money for a recognized charity

226 *Would you* **druther** *be*

- . . . a patch on a quilt handmade by Grandma for a new grandchild
- . . . the patch on the torn jeans of a rock star
- . . . a patch over the eye of a pirate

227 *If you were a movie star, would you* **druther** *meet your movie death by*

- . . . walking the plank
- . . . hanging from the highest tree
- . . . walking the "Green Mile"

228 *If you were a cat, would you **druther** be*

- . . . an alley cat adopted by a small child
- . . . a show cat with many ribbons
- . . . a much loved cartoon cat

229 *If you were a diamond ring,
would you **druther** be in*

- . . . a wedding set of a young bride
- . . . the ear stud of the sexiest man alive
- . . . the belly ring of the best known pop star

230 *Would you **druther** be a*

- . . . porch swing on the front porch of a southern home holding a young couple courting
- . . . child's swing in the city park
- . . . swing in a disco with a dancer on it

231 *If you were a drug, would you **druther** be a*

. . . painkilling drug used by a terminally ill
      patient for comfort

. . . drug to eliminate the side effects of a major
      muscular disease

. . . drug used to increase one's athletic ability

232 *Would you **druther** be forced to quit*

. . . smoking

. . . drinking

. . . gambling

233 *Would you **druther** have a*

. . . Super Bowl ring

. . . magical ring with super powers

. . . Bishop's ring

234 *If you were a young child, would you druther visit*

. . . your favorite grandmother's house

. . . a theme park

. . . a tree house built by your dad

235 *Would you druther travel to the*

. . . North Pole

. . . South Pole

. . . Equator

236 *If you were a movie, would you druther be a*

. . . popular DVD movie played by college kids

. . . classic kiddie video rental

. . . movie shown at the theater

237 *If you were a garden, would you **druther** be a*

 . . . vegetable garden grown in the inner city by school children

 . . . flower garden grown by a loving elderly lady

 . . . herb garden grown for research

238 *Would you **druther** be a*

 . . . commemorative stamp of a famous person

 . . . postage stamp on a lover's letter

 . . . country stamp on a passport

239 *If you were a passenger on a space shuttle, would you **druther** be the*

 . . . astronaut

 . . . paying celebrity guest traveler

 . . . classroom teacher

240 *If you were to recognize the most influential person in your life, would you druther honor*

. . . a teacher who turned on the learning light

. . . a mentor responsible for your professional success

. . . an encouraging family member

Our discussion on this one included lots of names being tossed out as we narrowed our choices. As we went through this question, we realized how blessed we have been.

Linda: I would choose mentor, because family members and teachers help you reach a certain point in life, but mentors help you reach goals in a chosen area.

Annetta: An encouraging family member. My father was very encouraging to me and told me that I could be whatever I wanted to be.

Ann: Teacher. I was blessed with a lot of good teachers.

Cathy: Encouraging family member. I had a wonderful aunt who encouraged me on many paths in life.

Bev: Teacher. Frances Coker helped me to totally turn my life around and to believe in myself.

241 *Would you **druther** have a*

... sleek and toned physique

... dynamite personality

... photographic memory

242 *If you were an archaeologist, would you **druther** work in*

... Mayan ruins

... the Egyptian tombs

... Native American mounds

243 *Would you **druther** be a*

... fat kindergarten pencil being used by a small child learning to write

... slim pencil behind the ear of a young man flirting with his high school sweetheart

... graphite pencil of an engineer designing a bridge

244 **W**ould you **druther** *be a tree*

   . . . holding a child's tree house

   . . . shading the porch of a home

   . . . whose wood is used to make a
        world-famous violin

245 **W**ould you **druther** *be a*

   . . . full-time homemaker

   . . . full-time career person

   . . . part-time worker

246 **W**ould you **druther** *see*

   . . . the world at peace

   . . . the environment saved

   . . . hunger abolished

247 *Would you **druther** work at*

- . . . one job you really loved all your life

- . . . many jobs you loved at different times in your life

- . . . a job you loved some of the time with someone you love

248 *Would you **druther** be a*

- . . . red sports car

- . . . silver family van

- . . . off-road hunting vehicle

249 *Would you **druther** be a*

- . . . soft couch in a therapist's office

- . . . leather sofa in a business professional's office

- . . . sofa bed in a house with frequent guests

250 *Would you **druther** be a*

    . . . telephone book for a large city

    . . . college catalog at a major university

    . . . tourist guidebook for a state

251 *If you were a cell phone, would you **druther** belong to a*

    . . . teenager

    . . . business person

    . . . politician

252 *Would you **druther** be*

    . . . a beauty queen

    . . . the queen of a country

    . . . a drag queen

253 *Would you* **druther** *be*

. . . mind

. . . body

. . . spirit

254 *Would you* **druther** *be*

. . . an owl

. . . an eagle

. . . a song bird

255 *In a park, would you* **druther** *be*

. . . soft, green grass under bare feet

. . . giant trees shading and singing in the breeze

. . . an inviting bench

?

256 *W*ould you **druther** be

... a candle to give light when the electricity is
   off during a storm

... an altar candle in a church

... a candle in a vigil march

257 *I*f you were an alphabetic letter,
*would you **druther** be on a*

... sign in Times Square

... famous movie marquee

... hand-inscribed old document

258 *W*ould you **druther** hear the

... song of a song bird

... music of a classical composition

... voices of children playing

259 *W*ould you **druther** be captured

. . . by a still camera

. . . by a video camera

. . . on a canvas

260 *W*ould you **druther** worry about

. . . children

. . . money

. . . spouse or significant other

261 *W*ould you **druther** hear

. . . windchimes

. . . a doorbell

. . . a bell on a cat's collar

?

262 *Would you **druther** visit with an old, school buddy using*

... email

... cell phone

... a handwritten letter

263 *Would you **druther** vacation in a*

... high-rise condo

... rustic cabin

... Holiday Inn® hotel

264 *Would you **druther** put a quarter in*

... an old-fashioned jukebox

... a slot machine

... a parking meter outside a museum

265 *Would you* **druther** *first explore a new culture by*

. . . reading extensively

. . . experiencing it first hand

. . . watching travel shows

266 *Would you* **druther** *be a*

. . . word

. . . symbol

. . . musical note

267 *If you were stranded on a deserted island for a month with food, water and shelter, would you* **druther** *have*

. . . moisturizer

. . . a companion

. . . a laptop computer

268 *Would you* **druther**

- . . . turn the other cheek
- . . . fight
- . . . get quiet revenge

269 *If you overheard a crime being planned, would you* **druther**

- . . . stay quiet and safe
- . . . report it anonymously to the authorities
- . . . intervene

270 *Which statement would you* **druther** *adopt as your own?*

- . . . variety is the spice of life
- . . . a good name is better to be had than great riches
- . . . be young, be foolish, be happy

271 *Would you **druther** live in a*

   . . . clear glass tumbler

   . . . stained glass box

   . . . cobalt blue vase

272 *Would you **druther** have*

   . . . tired feet

   . . . tired eyes

   . . . tired back

273 *Would you **druther** be a*

   . . . steel beam supporting a large bridge

   . . . wooden pole supporting a fishing deck

   . . . concrete slab supporting a family home

274 *Would you **druther** be a boat*

. . . rented out as a party barge

. . . owned by a weekend fisherman

. . . used as a ferry

275 *Would you **druther** cut*

. . . hair

. . . the lawn

. . . fabric

276 *After work, would you **druther***

. . . try a new restaurant

. . . go to an old favorite restaurant where the staff knows you

. . . go home and prepare something to eat

277 *If you were given $50, would you **druther***

... keep it

... return it for a choice of two envelopes, one empty and one containing $500

... give it to charity

278 *When under stress, would you **druther***

... be outside alone

... be with a friend at a coffee shop

... crawl into bed with a book

279 *In an embarrassing situation, would you **druther** be saved by*

... a stranger

... a family member

... an acquaintance from work

?

280 *W*ould you **druther** have lived in the

   ... wild west of Dale Evans

   ... roaring 20s of Zelda

   ... days of Scarlet O'Hara

This one had us laughing out loud as we envisioned each other in the life selected.

Annetta: Wild west because of the western influence in my life. I always wanted to be Belle Starr.
Linda: The Roaring 20's. I want to get out there and dance and flap.
Ann: The wild west of Dale Evans. I love westerns.
Cathy: Scarlet O'Hara days but I'd have to be a male. I wouldn't want to be cinched up.
Bev: The Roaring 20's. From what I've seen on television, it looked like a fun time.

281 Would you *druther* watch a

. . . romantic movie

. . . action movie

. . . scary movie

282 Would you *druther*

. . . sit alone in a comfortable chair reading

. . . sit on opposite ends of a sofa talking to a close friend

. . . snuggle with someone special on a love seat in front of the fireplace

283 Would you *druther* be

. . . intelligent

. . . the life of the party

. . . drop dead gorgeous

284 *Would you druther be*

... playing with your child
... visiting with your friend
... watching televison or reading by yourself

285 *Would you druther*

... sleep and dream
... sleep only
... stay awake

286 *Would you druther travel with the*

... circus
... fair
... rodeo

287 **W**ould *you* **druther** *watch*

. . . The History Channel

. . . Animal Planet

. . . a show on The Biography Channel

288 **O**n *a controversial issue, would you* **druther**

. . . speak up and take a strong vocal stand

. . . stay home and avoid the issue all together

. . . attend a public meeting but remain silent

289 **W**ould *you* **druther** *give up*

. . . the daily newspaper

. . . your computer

. . . your television

?

290 *Would you **druther** be a sign saying*

... WELCOME TO MY GARDEN

... BEWARE OF DOG

... POSTED - KEEP OUT

291 *If you were a stick of wood, would you **druther**
be burned at a*

... wiener roast

... college bonfire

... home fireplace as the yule log

292 *If you were a flower, would you **druther** be*

... a perennial

... an annual

... a weed

293 *Would you druther be*

- ... the crocus that blooms in early spring
- ... a day lily that flowers for one day and is gone
- ... a marigold that blooms all summer

294 *Would you druther*

- ... wear stylish shoes
- ... wear comfortable shoes
- ... go barefooted

295 *Would you druther have a*

- ... manicured flower garden
- ... cottage-style garden
- ... field of wildflowers

296 *Would you **druther** feel the*

. . . sun on your back

. . . wind in your face

. . . rain on your head

297 *To take care of you, would you **druther** have*

. . . your spouse

. . . an efficient maid

. . . your mother

298 *For spiritual renewal, would you **druther** have a*

. . . night alone under the stars

. . . morning alone in the sunshine

. . . quiet midday alone under the shade of a tree

299 *Would you **druther** be*

- ... wind chimes dancing in the backyard
- ... a storm siren warning people of danger
- ... church bells calling people to prayer

300 *Would you **druther** be*

- ... a firefighter
- ... a law officer
- ... an emergency technician

301 *If you had to solve a crime, would you **druther** be the*

- ... responding investigator
- ... detective investigating the crime
- ... chemist analyzing material

302 Would you **druther** clean

- . . . houses during the day
- . . . office buildings at night
- . . . automobiles on the weekend

303 Would you **druther**

- . . . work on a road-building crew in the mountains
- . . . be a steel-worker framing a skyscraper
- . . . frame individual homes in the suburbs

304 If you were a computer, would you **druther** be a

- . . . desktop computer
- . . . laptop
- . . . palm pilot

?

305 *Would you **druther** talk to a client*

   . . . in person at your office

   . . . in person at their home

   . . . over the telephone

306 *Would you **druther***

   . . . take pictures

   . . . develop film

   . . . frame photos

307 *As a creative writer, would you **druther** use*

   . . . a pencil with an eraser

   . . . an ink pen

   . . . a word processor

?

308 *To water your lovely flower garden, would you druther use*

... an automated sprinkler system

... a water hose

... a beautiful copper watering can

309 *Would you druther live in*

... a beautiful spacious home in a crime-infested area that is five minutes from your job

... a moderate house in a safe area that is forty-five minutes from your job

... an apartment in a gated complex that is twenty minutes from your job

310 *If you were a window washer, would you druther wash*

... windows in individual homes

... windows in high-rise buildings

... car windshields

311 *Would you* **druther**

- . . . please your parents
- . . . please your friends
- . . . please yourself

312 *Would you* **druther**

- . . . see the doctor annually for a check up, even though you are feeling fine
- . . . schedule doctor visits only when you've tried all home remedies and nothing has worked
- . . . schedule a doctor's appointment only when you feel sick

313 *When dealing with a personal problem, would you* **druther**

- . . . seek professional help
- . . . seek advice from a friend or family member
- . . . deal with it by yourself

314 **W**ould you **druther** sing

 . . . in a choir

 . . . in the shower

 . . . solo for an audience

315 **W**ould you **druther** shop

 . . . alone in the mall

 . . . with a friend at the mall

 . . . over the internet

316 **I**n dealing with a social problem that you believe calls for a change in societal attitudes, actions and beliefs, would you **druther**

 . . . join an organized group that works for change

 . . . write letters to politicians in power

 . . . talk about the issue, but never take overt action

317 *When putting flowers into your home or office, would you* **druther**

- . . . make an arrangement of beautiful, permanent flowers
- . . . buy fresh flowers at the market
- . . . cut flowers that you have grown in your own garden

318 *Would you* **druther**

- . . . make money
- . . . save money
- . . . spend money

319 *Would you* **druther** *be*

- . . . the father of the bride
- . . . the mother of the bride
- . . . the caterer

320 *If you could erase one thing from your past, would you **druther** erase*

. . . your academic record

. . . a failed romance

. . . your most embarrassing moment

We had fun with embarrassing moments and laughed at the ones we were willing to share!

Annetta: Failed romance.
Cathy: Most embarrassing moment. You don't want to know!
Linda: Most embarrassing moment.
Ann: Most embarrassing moment.
Bev: I'll erase my academic record. I don't like the idea of being judged by my grades.

321 *When making purchases, would you **druther***

. . . pay cash

. . . use a credit card

. . . write a check or use a debit card

322 *When you indulge yourself with something comforting, would you **druther** choose*

. . . food

. . . music

. . . sleep

323 *If you choose a food for comfort, would you **druther** have*

. . . potato chips

. . . chocolate

. . . ice cream

324 *If you listen to music to soothe your soul, would you* **druther** *choose*

. . . religious chants

. . . soft rock from the 60s, 70s and 80s

. . . surf or other water sounds

325 *Would you* **druther** *adopt a*

. . . pedigreed kitten purchased from an individual

. . . kitten selected from a litter available for free in front of a grocery store

. . . kitten from the animal shelter

326 *Would you* **druther** *work in an industry that*

. . . rarely changes and has few technological innovations

. . . undergoes rapid technological changes and requires constant on the job training

. . . undergoes moderate amounts of change which requires limited adaptation of new procedures

327 **W**ould you **druther** select a book that

   . . . makes you laugh

   . . . makes you cry

   . . . almost scares you to death

328 **W**ould you **druther**

   . . . weed your garden

   . . . clean your house

   . . . work at home

329 **T**o pamper yourself, would you **druther** have a

   . . . facial

   . . . manicure

   . . . massage

330 *Would you druther*

. . . watch a movie on the big screen

. . . go to a live play at the theater

. . . rent a video

331 *When you feel strongly about an issue and would like others to know how you feel, would you druther*

. . . put a bumper sticker on your car

. . . post your views on the web

. . . let others know your position in quiet ways on an individual basis

332 *When you need to know a telephone number, would you druther*

. . . look in the phone book

. . . call information

. . . look it up on the internet

333 *W*hen you are paying your monthly bills,
would you **druther**

- ... write and mail a check
- ... have an automatic draft
- ... pay it via the internet

334 *I*f you need information on a topic,
would you **druther**

- ... go to the local library
- ... go to a local bookstore
- ... look it up on the internet

335 *W*hen purchasing electronic equipment,
would you **druther**

- ... buy the most economical model available
  at a discount store
- ... shop on-line and wait for the equipment to be
  mailed to you
- ... spare no expense and purchase the latest
  gadgets instantly from a local electronics store

336 *When it comes to your expenditures, would you **druther***

   . . . spend your money freely

   . . . use a highly structured budget that accounts for every penny

   . . . have a flexible budget

337 *When you walk into a breathtakingly, well-decorated room, would you **druther** see*

   . . . smooth clean lines

   . . . antiques

   . . . country decor

338 *Would you **druther** be stuck in*

   . . . traffic

   . . . the mud

   . . . your job

?

339 *W*ould you **druther** drive on a

   . . . beautiful mountain road with hairpin curves

   . . . dirt road in the woods

   . . . cobblestone road in an ancient city

340 *W*ould you **druther** be tucked in at night with a

   . . . chocolate on your pillow

   . . . love note

   . . . hug from a child

341 *I*f you were a piece of old furniture,
would you **druther** be

   . . . standing in a flea market to be sold

   . . . dismantled for your beautiful hardware

   . . . left in an abandoned house to be discovered

342 *If you were a highway sign, would you **druther** read*

... WRONG WAY

... STOP

... SLIPPERY WHEN WET

343 *Would you **druther** your tombstone read*

... did it my way

... job well done

... I told you so

344 *Would you **druther** be a*

... helicopter

... tank

... Hummer®

?

345 *If you were a delicious fruit for sale, would you **druther** be sold*

- . . . on the side of the road by a man in a pick-up truck
- . . . at a neighborhood fruit stand
- . . . at a grocery market of organically grown fruits

346 *If you were a highway sign, would you **druther** read*

- . . . SPEED LIMIT 70
- . . . DETOUR
- . . . ROAD CLOSED

347 *If you were a cloud, would you **druther** be*

- . . . fluffy and white, forming an animal in the sky for a child lying in the grass
- . . . a full rain cloud bursting forth on farmers who had been praying for rain
- . . . a cloud allowing a beautiful red sunset to shine on the beach for lovers sitting on the pier

348 *If you had another life to live,
would you **druther** have more*

 ... freedom

 ... patience

 ... ambition

349 *Would you **druther** be a*

 ... slogan

 ... motto

 ... commandment

350 *Would you **druther** be a*

 ... rose in a parade float

 ... bead in a Mardi Gras necklace

 ... wart on a Halloween mask

351 *Would you **druther** be a*

- ... school bus carrying a load of children to the fair
- ... tour bus carrying tourists through wine country
- ... city bus taking its regular riders to their job

352 *Would you **druther** be a storage*

- ... building for antiques
- ... trunk for a bride-to-be
- ... bin for art supplies

353 *Would you **druther** drive*

- ... on an overpass
- ... in a tunnel
- ... on an exit ramp

354 *If you were a songbird, would you **druther** be in a*

. . . cage in a home with a loving owner

. . . large aviary visited by many people

. . . rain forest with other birds

355 *If you had a friend with a terminal illness, would you **druther** feel*

. . . relief that she will soon be out of pain

. . . guilty that you are well

. . . sadness for the loss of her friendship

356 *Would you **druther** be a truck hauling*

. . . fruits and vegetables

. . . new cars

. . . household furniture

357 *Would you **druther** have a job where you*

- ... travel all week to exotic places
- ... do not travel and stay in the comfort of your office
- ... travel within your own area by your own schedule

358 *Would you **druther** have your groceries bagged in*

- ... plastic
- ... paper
- ... your canvas bag

359 *While attending a Halloween party, would you **druther***

- ... wear a mask with your costume so no one knows who you are
- ... simply wear a costume
- ... wear street clothes

360 *Would you **druther** clean up*

... a junkyard of cars

... litter on the highway

... a refuse dump

361 *Would you **druther** your perfect date be a*

... candlelight dinner in a five-star restaurant with soft music playing

... starlight picnic on a secluded beach of white sand with a bonfire

... simple meal for two in a cabin with a mountain view and a crackling fire in the fireplace

362 *While planning a wedding, would you **druther** spend money on*

... lavish church appointments and the reception

... a month-long honeymoon after a civil ceremony

... a large down payment on a house

363 **W**ould you **druther** reconcile with

   . . . an estranged friend

   . . . a family member

   . . . a coworker

364 **W**ould you **druther** be a

   . . . country music star

   . . . classical jazz pianist

   . . . pop rock star

365 **W**ould you **druther** be a winner on

   . . . The Weakest Link

   . . . Fear Factor

   . . . Jeopardy

?

366 *If you were a flashing light,
would you **druther** be on*

   ... an ambulance

   ... a police car

   ... a road sign warning motorist the bridge is out

367 *If you were to see America,
would you **druther** see it by*

   ... biking

   ... motorcycling

   ... driving in a convertible

368 *If you were a church, would you **druther** be a*

   ... large and well-known cathedral

   ... a little church in the wildwood

   ... a television church

369 *If you had to decide on someone's punishment for a horrible crime, would you druther*

- ... set a death penalty
- ... give life in prison
- ... require a life time of work to repay the victim's family

370 *Would you druther be a junkyard*

- ... dog
- ... car for parts
- ... dealer

371 *Would you druther be a*

- ... billboard on the highway
- ... flashing portable sign
- ... a sign in Times Square

372 *Would you **druther** travel across America with*

. . . your six kids

. . . your complaining grandparents

. . . your angry ex-spouse

373 *Would you **druther** be a rose in*

. . . a groom's lapel

. . . the Kentucky Derby winner's blanket

. . . the tattoo of a famous star

374 *Would you **druther** be*

. . . Mary with her little lamb

. . . Little Miss Muffett with her little spider

. . . Snow White with her seven dwarfs

375 *Would you **druther** your knight in shining armor be*

. . . a cowboy

. . . an entrepreneur

. . . a surfer

376 *Would you **druther***

. . . pass all the cars on the highway without penalty

. . . drive the speed limit

. . . drive slowly and enjoy the scenery

377 *If you had financial difficulty, would you **druther***

. . . ask your parents for help

. . . sell some assets

. . . take a second or third job

378 *If you were a sign on a store, would you **druther** read*

... OPEN

... CLOSED

... BEING REMODELED

379 *Would you **druther** be*

... navy blues on a famous general

... sultry blues notes of a soulful blues man

... Blue's Clues

380 *Would you **druther** be a*

... checkered flag at a race

... national flag

... flag marking a location

381 *If you were a letter of the alphabet, would you druther be*

... A

... M

... Z

382 *Would you druther be a*

... domestic cat

... lion at the zoo

... free and wild leopard

383 *Would you druther*

... move north

... move south

... stay where you are

384 *Would you druther be*

. . . a famous person

. . . an impersonator of the famous

. . . a manager of a famous person

385 *Would you druther lose*

. . . faith

. . . hope

. . . love

386 *Would you druther receive*

. . . a diamond

. . . an emerald

. . . a ruby

387 **W**ould you **druther** teach

. . . kindergarten

. . . seventh grade

. . . college

388 **W**ould you **druther**

. . . read the newspaper

. . . watch the news on television

. . . be clueless about current events

389 **W**ould you **druther** have a

. . . maid

. . . cook

. . . chauffeur

?

390 *Would you druther*

- ... be six inches shorter
- ... be six inches taller
- ... remain as you are

391 *Would you druther bring in a New Year*

- ... at a gala event
- ... at home watching Dick Clark
- ... asleep in your bed

392 *Would you druther meet*

- ... George W. Bush
- ... Bill Clinton
- ... Jimmy Carter

393 *Would you druther*

... shovel stalls in a barn

... clean hotel rooms

... ride on a garbage truck

394 *Would you druther fight*

... fires

... crime

... battles

395 *If you were eligible to go to war for the U.S.A., would you druther*

... sign up for duty immediately

... take your chances at being called to duty

... skip the country

396 *Would you **druther** your Valentine*

   . . . bring you strawberries and cappuccino in bed

   . . . create a rose petal path that leads you to a
        steamy mineral bath

   . . . give you a massage with a delightful scented
        oil from head to toe on new luscious linens

397 *When visiting Aspen, Colorado,
would you **druther***

   . . . ski the slopes

   . . . shop at the boutiques

   . . . cuddle in a condo

398 *Would you **druther***

   . . . fly a kite

   . . . make a kite

   . . . be a kite

399 *If you thought your lover was being unfaithful, would you **druther** your best friend*

 . . . say nothing

 . . . tell the truth

 . . . drop hints that something is amiss

Before we read the final choice, Cathy shouted "tell the truth," and we were off and running! We were split between two answers. No one discussed the third choice.

Annetta: I would want them to say nothing.
Cathy: I'd want my best friend to tell the truth.
Linda: Tell the truth. I might briefly turn on my friend, but then I could deal with the issue.
Ann: I'd want my friend to say nothing. Ignorance is bliss. I might turn on the friend even if the affair is really happening, but I would hope it would be a short-term reaction.
Bev: Tell the truth, because I would feel betrayed by both people if I found out the truth on my own.

400 *Would you* **druther** *go*

 ... to a parade

 ... on a picnic

 ... to a party

401 *For Lent, would you* **druther** *give up*

 ... alcohol

 ... chocolate

 ... profanity

402 *On April Fool's Day, would you* **druther**

 ... play a joke on someone

 ... have one played on you

 ... cancel the holiday

?

403 *If you were a child, would you **druther** find*

. . . an Easter basket already prepared with goodies

. . . an empty basket ready to be taken on an
Easter egg hunt

. . . a real bunny hopping around in the bushes

404 *Would you **druther** vacation in*

. . . summer

. . . spring or fall

. . . winter

405 *Would you **druther** have to remove from
your home a*

. . . small garter snake

. . . black widow spider

. . . wasp nest and its occupants

406 *Would you **druther** bait your fishing hook with*

. . . minnows

. . . worms

. . . crickets

407 *Would you **druther** eat*

. . . sushi

. . . escargot

. . . boiled okra

408 *If you saw someone being attacked by a shark and you were the only person on the beach, would you **druther***

. . . attempt to intervene

. . . wring your hands and scream

. . . run for help

409 **W**ould you **druther** get home by

. . . hitchhiking

. . . catching a bus

. . . calling a friend

410 **I**f you were leaving your office and came upon
a manila envelope marked top secret,
would you **druther**

. . . pick it up and peek inside

. . . turn it into the parking attendant the next
morning without peeking

. . . leave it on the floor

411 **F**or the Fourth of July, would you **druther**

. . . attend a public fireworks display

. . . shoot your own fireworks

. . . sell fireworks

412 Would you *druther*

. . . raise your own vegetables

. . . buy vegetables at the Farmer's Market

. . . buy vegetables at the grocery store

413 *If you were a student, would you* **druther**

. . . wear a uniform

. . . have no dress code

. . . have a dress code with a few restrictions

414 Would you **druther** *be a*

. . . quarterback

. . . cheerleader

. . . coach

415 *If you knew you were going to be saved, would you druther be*

... trapped in an air pocket under a boat in cold water

... hanging from a teetering rope in the wind while mountain climbing

... lost in a dark cave

We talked about this one in great depth. Most of our emotion was centered around the tough, negative choices we had to make.

Annetta: Air pocket in the cold water. I have a fear of heights so I could not be dangling.

Cathy: I'm going to hang from that rope. I'd rather be dry and cold than wet and cold.

Linda: Air pocket in the cold water. I couldn't dangle. I'm like Annetta about heights.

Ann: I'll dangle, let the wind move me and enjoy the great view.

Bev: I'm going to dangle from the rope. It would be easier for the rescue team to see me.

LINDA   CATHY
        ANN
BEV   ANNETTA

*We appreciate your willingness to
share this journey with us.
If you have comments or thoughts
you would like to pass along to
The Druthers Sisters regarding*
The Book of Druthers,
please visit
www.**drutherssisters**.com
or send correspondence to:
The Druthers Sisters
P. O. Box 2581
Jackson, MS 39207-2581